JIMMY SNIFFLES
DOGNAPPED!

raintree
a Capstone company — publishers for children

Raintree is an imprint of Capstone Global Library Limited, a company incorporated in England and Wales having its registered office at 264 Banbury Road, Oxford, OX2 7DY – Registered company number: 6695582

www.raintree.co.uk
myorders@raintree.co.uk

Text © Capstone Global Library Limited 2020
The moral rights of the proprietor have been asserted.

Designed by Heather Kindseth and Keegan Gilbert
Original illustrations © Capstone Global Library Limited 2020
Originated by Capstone Global Library Ltd
Printed and bound in India

978 1 4747 9187 8 (paperback)

British Library Cataloguing in Publication Data
A full catalogue record for this book is available from the British Library.

JiMMY SNiFFLES
DOGNAPPED!

BY SCOTT NICKEL

ILLUSTRATED BY STEVE HARPSTER

CAST OF CHARACTERS

Scurvy the Clown

Jimmy Sniffles

Petey the Poodle

Petey's Pals

Mrs Beasley

Jimmy dashes outside to investigate.

A trail of perfume snakes its way from the woman to Jimmy.

Man, her perfume stinks!

ARF! ARF!

13

14

ACHOOO!

Why am I still sneezing? It's just a clown and that lady over the road.

23

27

ABOUT THE AUTHOR

Scott Nickel works by day at Paws, Inc., Jim Davis's famous Garfield studio, and he freelances by night. Burning the midnight oil, Scott has created hundreds of humorous greeting cards and written several children's books, short fiction for *Boys' Life* magazine, comic strips and lots of really funny knock-knock jokes. He has also eaten a lot of midnight snacks. Scott lives in Indiana, USA, where with his wife, two sons, six cats and several sea monkeys.

ABOUT THE ILLUSTRATOR

Steve Harpster has loved drawing funny cartoons, mean monsters and goofy gadgets since he was able to pick up a pencil. When he was little, instead of writing a report about a dog-sledge story set in Alaska, Steve made a comic book about it. He was worried the teacher might not like it, but she hung it up for all the children in the class to see. "It taught me to take a chance and try something different," says Steve. Steve got a job drawing funny pictures for books. He used to be an animator for Disney. Now, Steve lives in Ohio, USA, with his wonderful wife, Karen, and their sheepdog, Doodle.

GLOSSARY

harumph noise adults make when you sneeze and forget to cover your mouth

mangy messy and having hair in knots. Actually, it's the way you or your dog look just before taking a bath.

sludge dirty, gloppy, mucky stuff

Super Sinus 6000 Booger Zooka perfect weapon for loading and throwing snot at villains

CLOWN CLUES

Being a clown is serious business!

The biggest number of clowns ever gathered in one place at one time is 850. That's a lot of red noses!

The fear of clowns is known as coulrophobia.

Clowns consider it bad luck to use blue face paint.

The word *clown* comes from the word *clod*, which means "a clumsy person".

Clown Alley is the name of the area in a circus where clowns get dressed and put on their make-up.

Until 1998 there was an actual clown college. Graduates were guaranteed a job in the famous Barnum and Bailey Circus.

It can take a clown up to two hours to apply face make-up. Most clowns make sure that none of their real skin shows.

Most circuses are performed inside rings and are hosted by a ringmaster. That's because the first circuses were performed in ancient Rome in giant circular stadiums. "Circus" is the Roman word for "circle".

Why don't the circus lions eat the clowns?
Because the clowns taste funny!

DISCUSSION QUESTIONS

1. When did you think that Mrs Beasley was up to no good? What sort of clues did the writer give you?

2. Scurvy the Clown only wants to begin his own amazing dog circus. Does this really make him a villain?

3. If you were Jimmy, how would you have helped rescue the dogs from Mrs Beasley and Scurvy the Clown?

ACHOOO!

WRITING PROMPTS

1. Jimmy's nose always alerts him to trouble. Do you have anything that alerts you to trouble? If so, what is it?

2. Oh no, someone new just moved in next door to you and they are up to something evil! What exactly are they up to, and how are you going to stop them?

3. There are a lot of sound effects in this story. That's one way writers make the story come to life. Describe how the story would be different if there were no sound effects. How else would you know what a Super Sinus 6000 sounded like? Choose three pages with great sounds and replace them with sounds of your own.